simply
heaven

Published by Kraft Foods Limited,
187 Todd Road, Fishermans Bend, Victoria, Australia 3207.

Printed and bound in China by C&C Offset Printing Co., Ltd.,
a registered trading company in Hong Kong, Business
Registration Certificate number 11665156-000-03-07-5, 14/F.,
Ting Lai Road, C&C Building, Tai Po, N.T., Hong Kong.

KRAFT, PHILADELPHIA, PHILLY, TRY IT ON, OREO and TOBLERONE
are trademarks of Kraft Foods.

ISBN 978-0-646-51576-2

Layout and design by Lithocraft Pty Ltd, Truganina

simply
heaven

75 irresistible savoury and sweet PHILADELPHIA recipes for all occasions

contents

Simply Heaven shows you how to experiment with recipes that are a breeze to make. It's all about providing inspiration for everyday cooking and those special occasions when you want to impress.

The 75 irresistible recipes inside all share one key ingredient – PHILADELPHIA Cream Cheese. You will find that it's an incredibly versatile ingredient that is a lighter, creamier and healthier alternative to butter or cream.

PHILADELPHIA Cream Cheese has been a household favourite since its arrival in Australia in 1956. It originated in the United States and was named 'Philadelphia' after the city, which was famous for its high quality dairy goods. The PHILADELPHIA Cream Cheese recipe was first created by dairy farmer William A. Lawrence who started experimenting with cheeses in 1872 and the rest, as they say, is history!

Today, PHILADELPHIA Cream Cheese is proudly Australian made and produced in Mount Gambier, South Australia.

Simply Heaven includes added tips and hints that will make preparing appetisers, salads, light meals, dinners and desserts an absolute pleasure. It's a fabulous handbook for anyone who is looking for simple inspiration in the kitchen. Enjoy!

appetisers & salads

Carrot Dip with Oven Baked Pita Chips

Serves 8
Preparation time: 10 minutes
Cooking time: 20 minutes

3 carrots (400g), peeled and chopped
125g PHILADELPHIA Spreadable Light
   Cream Cheese
¼ cup grated Parmesan cheese
2 tablespoons milk
1 clove garlic, crushed
1½ teaspoons cumin
Salt and pepper, to taste

2 large pita breads, sliced into wedges
Olive oil spray

Chopped fresh chives, for garnish

1 Boil, microwave or steam carrots until tender. Place carrots in a food processor and process until smooth. Add PHILLY, Parmesan, milk, garlic, cumin and seasonings and process until well combined. Chill.

2 Place pita bread on a large baking tray and spray with oil. Bake in a hot oven 200°C for 5–10 minutes or until golden and crisp.

3 Spoon the dip into a serving bowl, sprinkle with chives. Serve with oven baked pita chips.

Spinach & White Bean Dip

Serves 8
Preparation time: 10 minutes
Cooking time: 10 minutes

1 tablespoon olive oil
1 large onion, finely chopped
2 cloves garlic, finely chopped
½ teaspoon fennel seeds
2 x 400g cans cannellini beans, rinsed
    and drained
50g baby spinach leaves
125g PHILADELPHIA Block Cream Cheese,
    softened
1 tablespoon lemon juice
Salt and pepper, to taste

Extra oil, for drizzling
Blanched vegetables, to serve
Lavosh, to serve

1 Heat oil in a heavy based saucepan, add onion, garlic and fennel and cook for 5–6 minutes until onion has softened.

2 Add the beans and spinach and cook a further 2–3 minutes. Remove from heat and allow to cool slightly.

3 Process the bean mixture, PHILLY, lemon juice and seasonings until smooth. Spoon the dip into a serving bowl, drizzle with extra oil and serve with blanched vegetables and lavosh.

Light & Creamy Sundried Tomato Dip

Serves 8
Preparation time: 10 minutes

220g PHILADELPHIA Spreadable Extra Light
   Cream Cheese
½ cup chopped semi sundried tomatoes
2 tablespoons chopped chives
2 cloves garlic, crushed
Salt and pepper, to taste
Extra chopped chives, for garnish

Turkish bread, to serve
Artichoke hearts, to serve
Marinated roasted red capsicum, to serve
Kalamata olives, to serve

1 Combine the PHILLY with tomatoes, chives, garlic and seasonings. Chill.
2 Spoon the dip into a serving bowl, sprinkle with extra chives. Serve on a platter with Turkish bread, artichokes, roasted capsicum and olives.

Salsa Con Queso

Serves 8
Preparation time: 5 minutes
Cooking time: 10 minutes

1½ cups tomato salsa
250g PHILADELPHIA Block Cream Cheese, chopped
2 tablespoons sweet chilli sauce
3–4 spring onions, chopped

Spring onions, extra, chopped for garnish
Corn chips, to serve

1 Heat the salsa in a saucepan, whisk in the PHILLY
and continue to whisk until smooth.

2 Stir in the chilli sauce and spring onions. Spoon
the dip into a serving bowl, sprinkle with extra spring
onions and serve warm or cold with corn chips.

Guacamole with Prawn Fritters

Makes 18
Preparation time: 25 minutes
Cooking time: 15 minutes

125g PHILADELPHIA Spreadable Light
  Cream Cheese
1 avocado, peeled and mashed
¼ cup chopped coriander
2 teaspoons grated lemon rind
1 tablespoon lemon juice
Salt and pepper, to taste

½ cup milk
1 egg
1½ tablespoons sweet chilli sauce
400g cooked prawns, peeled and chopped
1 cup self–raising flour, sifted
3 spring onions, chopped
2 tablespoons oil, for cooking

Extra coriander, for garnish

1 Combine the PHILLY, avocado, coriander, lemon rind, juice and seasonings. Spoon the dip into a serving bowl. Chill.

2 Whisk together the milk, egg and sweet chilli sauce. Stir through the prawns, flour, spring onions and season to taste.

3 Heat the oil in a large non–stick frypan and cook tablespoonsful of mixture over a medium heat for 2–3 minutes on each side until golden. Drain. Repeat with remaining mixture. Serve fritters warm with Guacamole and garnish with coriander.

Tomato & Balsamic Bruschetta

Serves 4
Preparation time: 15 minutes
Cooking time: 10 minutes

8 thick slices baguette, ciabatta or similar
Garlic olive oil spray

125g PHILADELPHIA Spreadable Light
  Cream Cheese
12 cherry tomatoes, halved
½ small red onion, very finely sliced
1 tablespoon balsamic vinegar
1 tablespoon olive oil
½ teaspoon brown sugar
Salt and pepper, to taste
Torn basil leaves, for garnish

1 Spray both sides of the baguette slices
with oil and toast under a grill or chargrill
until golden. Cool.

2 Spread the PHILLY over each slice of toast,
top with tomato and onion.

3 Whisk together the vinegar, oil, sugar and
seasonings, then drizzle over the tomatoes.
Garnish with basil. Serve immediately.

Mini Pumpkin & Cherry Tomato Quiches

Makes 12
Preparation time: 15 minutes
Cooking time: 35 minutes

300g butternut pumpkin, peeled and cut
    into 1cm cubes
Olive oil spray

12 slices white bread, crusts removed
12 cherry tomatoes, halved
125g PHILADELPHIA Spreadable Cream Cheese,
    softened
3 eggs
¼ cup cream
2 tablespoons chopped chives
Salt and pepper, to taste

1 Place pumpkin on a lined baking tray and spray with oil. Bake in a hot oven 200°C for 15 minutes or until tender.

2 Roll each slice of bread to flatten, then press into 12 × ⅓ cup capacity greased muffin pans. Spoon in the pumpkin and tomato.

3 Whisk the PHILLY, eggs, cream, chives and seasonings until smooth, then spoon evenly over the vegetables. Bake in a hot oven 200°C for 15–18 minutes until golden. Cool slightly, then remove and serve warm or cold.

Baked Mushrooms with Prosciutto

Makes 12
Preparation time: 15 minutes
Cooking time: 15 minutes

110g PHILADELPHIA Spreadable Extra Light
   Cream Cheese
1 clove garlic, crushed

12 medium mushroom caps, approx. 6cm
   with stalks removed
Garlic olive oil spray
Salt and pepper, to taste

100g prosciutto, grilled until crisp and broken
   into strips
Chopped chives, for garnish

1 Combine the PHILLY and garlic.
2 Place the mushrooms on a foil lined baking tray, stalk side up. Spray with oil and season to taste. Cook under a preheated grill, medium heat for 6–8 minutes until just tender. Allow to cool slightly.
3 Spoon a dollop of the PHILLY mixture onto the mushrooms, top with the prosciutto and a sprinkle of chives. Serve immediately.

Middle Eastern Lamb Pies

Makes 12
Preparation time: 25 minutes
Cooking time: 20 minutes

1 tablespoon olive oil
1 large onion, finely chopped
2 cloves garlic, crushed
500g lamb mince
2 teaspoons ground cumin
1 teaspoon cinnamon
¼ cup tomato paste
1 tablespoon flour
1 cup beef stock
Salt and pepper, to taste

6 sheets filo pastry
Garlic olive oil spray

125g PHILADELPHIA Spreadable Light
   Cream Cheese
¼ cup finely shredded mint
⅓ cup toasted pine nuts

1 Heat the oil in a frypan and sauté onion for
1–2 minutes until just softened. Add garlic and
lamb mince and cook for 5 minutes or until lamb
has browned. Add spices and tomato paste and
cook for 1 minute. Blend flour with the stock then
add to the lamb mixture. Simmer for 5–6 minutes
until thickened. Season to taste.

2 Spray a sheet of filo with oil, top with another
sheet and spray with oil. Fold sheets in half and
cut into 4 squares. Repeat with remaining filo. Push
filo pieces into 12 × ⅓ cup capacity greased muffin
pans, folding the edges in. Bake in a hot oven
200°C for 8–10 minutes or until golden.

3 Combine the PHILLY with half the mint. Spoon lamb
filling into the filo cases, dollop with PHILLY mixture
and sprinkle with remaining mint and pine nuts.
Serve immediately.

Zucchini Bites with Smoked Salmon

Makes 24
Preparation time: 15 minutes
Cooking time: 30 minutes

2 large (400g) zucchini, grated
1 onion, peeled and grated
250g PHILADELPHIA Spreadable Cream Cheese,
   softened
1 cup self–raising flour
½ cup grated tasty cheese
½ cup oil
5 eggs, lightly beaten
Salt and pepper, to taste

1 tablespoons finely chopped dill
Finely grated rind of 1 lemon
100g sliced smoked salmon, cut into strips
Dill sprigs

1 Drain excess moisture from the zucchini
and combine with onions, 100g of the PHILLY,
flour, cheese, oil, eggs and seasonings until
well combined.

2 Spoon the mixture into a greased and lined
22cm x 30cm pan. Bake in a moderate oven
180°C for 30 minutes or until firm to touch.
Allow to cool, then cut into 24 squares.

3 Combine the remaining PHILLY, dill and rind.
Top each square with a dollop of PHILLY mixture,
smoked salmon and dill. Serve immediately.

Asian Style Chicken & Cashew Cakes

Makes 15
Preparation time: 20 minutes
Cooking time: 20 minutes

500g chicken mince
1 red onion, finely chopped
125g PHILADELPHIA Block Cream Cheese,
  softened
½ cup roasted, salted cashews, finely chopped
⅓ cup chopped basil
⅓ cup chopped coriander
Finely grated rind of 1 large lemon
Plain flour, for rolling
Oil, for shallow frying

¼ cup white vinegar
¼ cup water
¼ cup brown sugar
1 tablespoon sweet chilli sauce
2 teaspoons fish sauce
1 tablespoon chopped cashews, extra
1 bird's eye chilli, sliced

15 basil leaves, extra

1 Combine mince, onion, PHILLY, cashews, herbs and lemon rind. Roll 2 tablespoons of the chicken mixture into a ball, then flatten slightly. Toss through flour until coated, shake off excess.

2 Heat the oil in a large non-stick frypan. Cook the cakes over medium heat for 6–8 minutes or until cooked through and golden brown. Drain and keep warm.

3 To make dipping sauce: combine vinegar, water, sugar, sweet chilli sauce, fish sauce, cashews and chilli in a saucepan and cook for 3–5 minutes until sugar is dissolved and sauce has thickened slightly. Place each chicken cake on a basil leaf and serve with dipping sauce.

Mediterranean Mini Toasts

Makes 24
Preparation time: 10 minutes

150g PHILADELPHIA Spreadable Light
  Cream Cheese
2 tablespoons chopped basil
1 clove garlic, crushed

ANCHOVY and CAPSICUM
12 mini bagel toasts
6 anchovy fillets, drained and halved
1 small roasted red capsicum, cut into 12 strips
Baby basil leaves, for garnish

SALAMI and TOMATO
12 mini lavosh or mini toasts
6 slices hot shaved salami, cut into strips
3 baby roma tomatoes, quartered
Baby basil leaves, for garnish

1 Combine the PHILLY, basil and garlic in a bowl.
2 Anchovy and Capsicum Toasts: spread toasts with half the PHILLY mixture and top with anchovies and capsicum. Garnish with basil leaves.
3 Salami and Tomato Toasts: spread lavosh with the remaining PHILLY mixture and top with salami and tomato. Garnish with basil leaves.

Goat's Cheese & Walnut Mini Cheesecakes

Makes 24
Preparation time: 25 minutes
Cooking time: 15 minutes

¾ cup fresh breadcrumbs
½ cup finely ground walnuts
30g butter, melted

250g PHILADELPHIA Block Cream Cheese,
  softened
200g fresh goat's cheese
2 eggs
2 tablespoons chopped fresh chives
Salt and pepper, to taste
Walnut pieces, for garnish
½ red capsicum, finely diced, for garnish

Chives, extra, for garnish

1 Combine the breadcrumbs, walnuts and butter. Spoon a heaped teaspoon into 24 greased mini muffin pans and press into the base.
2 Beat the PHILLY and goat's cheese until smooth, then beat in the eggs until well combined. Stir in the chives and seasonings and evenly divide mixture between the bases.
3 Top half the cheesecakes with a walnut piece and top remaining half with capsicum. Bake in a moderate oven 180°C for 15 minutes or until puffed and golden. Cool in pans for 5 minutes, then unmould. Garnish with extra chives and serve warm.

Oven Roasted Tomato, Broad Bean & Asparagus Salad

Serves 4
Preparation time: 15 minutes
Cooking time: 25 minutes

¼ cup white wine vinegar
¼ cup olive oil
1 teaspoon Dijon mustard
½ teaspoon sugar
Salt and pepper, to taste

125g PHILADELPHIA Block Cream Cheese,
   broken into 2cm pieces
125g mini Roma tomatoes, halved
250g frozen broad beans, blanched and peeled
2 bunches asparagus, blanched
½ cup fresh peas, blanched

1 Whisk together the vinegar, oil, mustard, sugar and seasonings to form a dressing. Place the PHILLY and tomatoes on a lined baking tray. Drizzle with 2 tablespoons of dressing.

2 Bake in a moderate oven 180°C for 15–20 minutes or until PHILLY is golden and tomatoes are slightly shrivelled. Cool.

3 Arrange the broad beans, asparagus and peas on a serving platter. Top with the PHILLY and tomatoes, drizzle with remaining dressing. Serve immediately.

Warm Potato, Parsnip & Artichoke Salad

Serves 4
Preparation time: 15 minutes
Cooking time: 30 minutes

800g baby chat potatoes, halved
4 medium parsnips, peeled and cut into
  5cm lengths
1 tablespoon olive oil
1 tablespoon chopped rosemary
Salt and pepper, to taste
400g can artichoke hearts, drained and halved

125g PHILADELPHIA Spreadable Light Cream
  Cheese
1 tablespoon honey
2 tablespoons milk
1 tablespoon seeded mustard
1 tablespoon roughly chopped flat–leaf parsley

Rosemary sprigs, for garnish

1 Combine potatoes, parsnips, oil, rosemary
and seasonings in a large bowl and toss to coat.
Place on a lined baking tray and bake in a very
hot oven 220°C for 25–30 minutes or until tender.
Place on a serving platter and toss through
the artichokes.
2 Whisk together the PHILLY, honey, milk and
mustard until smooth. Stir through the parsley
and drizzle over the vegetables. Garnish with
rosemary. Serve immediately.

Chargrilled Turkish Bread Salad

Serves 4
Preparation time: 15 minutes
Cooking time: 15 minutes

125g PHILADELPHIA Block Cream Cheese,
    broken into 2cm pieces
Olive oil spray
1 clove garlic, crushed
1 tablespoon grated lemon rind
Cracked pepper, to taste

2 Turkish bread rolls, halved horizontally
50g baby rocket leaves
1 large avocado, sliced
1 punnet grape tomatoes, halved

¼ cup balsamic vinegar
¼ cup olive oil
½ teaspoon sugar
Salt and pepper, to taste

1 Place the PHILLY on a lined baking tray. Spray with oil and sprinkle with garlic, lemon rind and pepper. Bake in a hot oven 200°C for 10 minutes, until lightly browned. Allow to cool slightly.

2 Cut each piece of bread diagonally into three slices. Spray the bread with oil and chargrill until golden.

3 Arrange the bread, rocket, avocado, tomatoes and baked PHILLY on a serving platter, whisk together the vinegar, oil, sugar and seasonings and drizzle over the salad. Serve immediately.

Roast Pumpkin Salad
with Prosciutto & Beans

Serves 4
Preparation time: 20 minutes
Cooking time: 40 minutes

½ cup olive oil
2 cloves garlic, crushed
500g jap or kent pumpkin, peeled and cut into
   1cm thick slices
125g PHILADELPHIA Block Cream Cheese,
   broken into 2cm pieces

¼ cup balsamic vinegar
1 teaspoon brown sugar
Salt and pepper, to taste

100g prosciutto or bacon, fried until crisp
¾ cup cashews, toasted
150g green beans, blanched

1 Combine the oil, garlic and pumpkin and bake
in a roasting pan in a hot oven 200°C for 20 minutes
or until just tender. Add the PHILLY and bake for a
further 10 minutes or until PHILLY is golden. Cool for
5 minutes, drain and reserve garlic oil.

2 Whisk the garlic oil with vinegar, sugar and
seasonings for the dressing.

3 Arrange the pumpkin and PHILLY on a serving
platter, top with prosciutto, cashews and beans,
drizzle with the dressing. Serve immediately.

Roasted Beetroot & Macadamia Salad

Serves 4
Preparation time: 10 minutes
Cooking time: 30 minutes

3 large beetroot, washed and quartered
Olive oil spray

¼ cup lemon juice
¼ cup olive oil
1 tablespoon honey
Finely grated rind of 1 lemon
Salt and pepper, to taste

50g baby beetroot leaves
50g mixed salad leaves
½ cup macadamia nuts, roughly chopped
125g PHILADELPHIA Block Cream Cheese,
    crumbled

1 Place beetroot on a lined baking tray.
Spray with oil and bake in a hot oven 200°C
for 30 minutes or until tender.

2 Whisk together the lemon juice, oil, honey, rind
and seasonings to make the dressing.

3 Arrange leaves, nuts and beetroot on a serving
platter. Top with PHILLY and drizzle with dressing.
Serve immediately.

Beef Salad with Chilli, Mint & Coriander Dressing

Serves 4
Preparation time: 15 minutes
Cooking time: 15 minutes

250g PHILADELPHIA Block Cream Cheese
Olive oil spray

400g lean porterhouse steak

100g lettuce mix
150g baby corn, blanched and cut
  in half lengthways
150g green beans, blanched
1 red onion, cut into thin wedges

¼ cup sweet chilli sauce
2 tablespoons white vinegar
2 tablespoons oil
2 tablespoons chopped mint
2 tablespoons chopped coriander
1 teaspoon grated lime or lemon rind

¼ cup roasted unsalted peanuts, for garnish

1 Cut the PHILLY into ten slices, then halve each slice diagonally. Place the PHILLY triangles on a lined baking tray. Spray with oil and bake in a hot oven 200°C for 10 minutes or until golden.

2 Chargrill or barbecue the steak for 5–8 minutes, or to your liking. Allow to rest 3 minutes before thinly slicing.

3 Arrange the lettuce, corn, beans, onion, PHILLY and beef on serving plates. Whisk together the chilli sauce, vinegar, oil, herbs and lemon rind to form a dressing. Drizzle over the salad and scatter with peanuts. Serve immediately.

light meals

Creamy Leek & Potato Soup

Serves 4
Preparation time: 15 minutes
Cooking time: 30 minutes

20g butter
2 leeks, halved lengthways, sliced
2 cloves garlic, crushed
4 cups chicken stock
600g potatoes, peeled and chopped
125g PHILADELPHIA Spreadable Light
  Cream Cheese
½ cup milk
Salt and pepper, to taste

1/4 cup chopped chives, for garnish
100g thinly sliced pepperoni, fried until crisp
  and drained, for garnish
Crusty bread, to serve

1 Heat the butter in a large heavy-based
saucepan. Add the leek and garlic and sauté for
5 minutes until softened. Add the stock and potato
then cook, covered for 10–15 minutes or until
potato is tender. Blend or process the soup until
smooth then return to the saucepan.

2 Whisk the PHILLY and milk into the soup until
smooth, simmer for a further 5 minutes until heated,
season to taste. Ladle into serving bowls and garnish
with a sprinkle of chives and crispy pepperoni,
serve with crusty bread. Serve immediately.

Roasted Sweet Potato & Garlic Soup

Serves 6
Preparation time: 15 minutes
Cooking time: 30 minutes

1kg sweet potato (kumera), peeled and chopped
1 onion, roughly chopped
1 head garlic, broken into cloves and peeled
1 tablespoon olive oil
6 cups chicken stock
250g PHILADELPHIA Spreadable Light
   Cream Cheese
Salt and pepper, to taste

Parsley, for garnish
Chargrilled ciabatta, to serve

1 Toss the sweet potato, onion, and garlic in oil.
Place on a lined oven tray and bake in a hot oven
200°C for 20–25 minutes or until tender.

2 Place roasted vegetables in a large saucepan
with stock and bring to the boil. Remove from the
heat and allow to cool slightly. Blend or process
the soup until smooth then return to the saucepan.

3 Whisk the PHILLY into the soup until smooth,
simmer for a further 5 minutes until well heated.
Season to taste then ladle into serving bowls
and garnish with parsley. Serve immediately.

Potato Rosti with Lemon Cream & Smoked Salmon

Serves 4
Preparation time: 20 minutes
Cooking time: 20 minutes

125g PHILADELPHIA Spreadable Light
  Cream Cheese
1 tablespoon chopped dill
Grated rind of 1 lemon

600g potatoes, peeled and grated
1 onion, peeled and finely grated
⅓ cup oil
Salt and pepper, to taste

100g sliced smoked salmon
¼ cup baby capers, for garnish
Extra dill sprigs, for garnish
Lemon wedges, for garnish

1 Mix together the PHILLY, dill and lemon rind.
Set aside.

2 Combine potatoes and onions and squeeze
out excess liquid. Heat one tablespoon of oil in
a large non-stick frypan over a medium heat,
add potato mixture and cook for 8 minutes, stirring
occasionally. Transfer mixture to a large bowl and
allow to cool. Season with salt and pepper, then
divide mixture into 8 and shape into patties.

3 Heat the remaining oil in a frypan and cook
rosti (in two batches if necessary) over a medium
heat for 3–4 minutes on each side or until crisp
and golden. Drain well.

4 Stack 2 rosti on each serving plate with the
smoked salmon. Dollop the rosti with lemon
cream and garnish with capers, dill and lemon
wedges. Serve immediately.

Frittata Primavera

Serves 4
Preparation time: 10 minutes
Cooking time: 30 minutes

100g spaghetti
6 eggs
250g PHILADELPHIA Spreadable Light
  Cream Cheese
1 bunch asparagus, trimmed, blanched
  and halved
1 cup frozen peas, thawed
½ cup basil leaves, chopped
2 spring onions, chopped
Salt and pepper, to taste

Basil leaves, for garnish
Shaved Parmesan, for garnish
Roasted cherry tomatoes, to serve

1 Cook the spaghetti in a large saucepan
of rapidly boiling water for 10–12 minutes until
al dente. Drain.

2 Whisk together the eggs and PHILLY until
smooth. Stir in the cooked pasta, asparagus,
peas, basil, spring onions and seasonings.

3 Pour into an oiled non–stick 24cm frypan and
cook over a low heat for 10–15 minutes until almost
cooked through. Place under a preheated grill
and cook for 3–5 minutes to brown the top and
finish cooking. Slice and place onto serving plates,
garnish with basil and Parmesan and serve with
roasted tomatoes. Serve immediately.

Ham, Artichoke & Parmesan Frittata

Serves 4
Preparation time: 15 minutes
Cooking time: 15 minutes

100g leg ham, sliced
400g can artichoke hearts, drained and halved
250g PHILADELPHIA Spreadable Cream Cheese, softened
4 eggs
¼ cup cream
1 tablespoon chopped thyme
¼ cup grated Parmesan cheese

Flat leaf parsley, for garnish
Salad greens, to serve

1 Arrange the ham and artichokes evenly over the base of a greased, non-stick 24cm frypan.

2 Whisk the PHILLY with eggs, cream and thyme, then pour over the ham and artichokes.

3 Cook the frittata over a medium heat for 8–10 minutes until almost cooked through. Sprinkle over the Parmesan then place under a preheated grill and cook for 3–5 minutes to brown the top and finish cooking. Slice the frittata and place onto serving plates, garnish with parsley and serve with salad greens. Serve immediately.

Blue Cheese Soufflé
with Polenta Crust

Serves 4
Preparation time: 20 minutes
Cooking time: 25 minutes

Olive oil spray
¼ cup polenta

30g butter
¼ cup flour
1 cup milk
4 eggs, separated
125g PHILADELPHIA Spreadable Light
   Cream Cheese
100g blue cheese, crumbled

Flat leaf parsley, for garnish

1 Lightly oil 4 x 1 cup capacity soufflé dishes, sprinkle with polenta and place on an oven tray.

2 Melt the butter in a saucepan, add flour and cook, stirring for 1 minute without colouring. Gradually add milk and whisk continuously until mixture boils and thickens. Transfer mixture to a large bowl. Stir in egg yolks, PHILLY and blue cheese. Allow to cool.

3 Beat the egg whites until stiff peaks form and gently fold whites through the cheese mixture. Divide mixture between the soufflé dishes. Bake in a hot oven 200°C for 15 minutes or until risen and lightly browned, garnish with parsley. Serve immediately.

Crêpes with Smoked Trout

Serves 4
Preparation time: 30 minutes
Cooking time: 15 minutes

½ cup flour
2 eggs
¾ cup milk
2 teaspoons oil

250g PHILADELPHIA Spreadable Cream Cheese
¼ cup light sour cream
¼ cup chopped chives
Grated rind and juice of 1 lime
TABASCO* sauce
1 medium whole smoked trout, skin and bones
   removed and broken into pieces

Chopped chives, for garnish
Green salad, for serving

1 Whisk together the flour, eggs, milk and oil to
form a smooth batter. Allow to stand for 30 minutes.

2 Pour 2–3 tablespoons of the mixture into a
greased, preheated crêpe pan. Cook the crêpe
until mixture is set on the top. Turn the crêpe over,
cook for a further minute or until golden. Continue
with remaining batter to make 8 crêpes.

3 Combine the PHILLY, sour cream, chives, lime
rind, juice, TABASCO* and trout. Divide the mixture
into eight then spread down the centre of each
crêpe. Roll gently to enclose the filling.

4 Arrange 2 crêpes on each serving plate
garnish with chives and serve with green salad.
Serve immediately.

*TABASCO is a trademark of McIlhenny Co.

Pesto Chicken Baguette

Makes 2
Preparation time: 10 minutes

110g PHILADELPHIA Spreadable Extra Light
   Cream Cheese
¼ cup basil pesto
1 x 30cm baguette or 2 small baguettes
   halved lengthways
20g baby spinach leaves
200g chicken breast fillet, cooked and sliced
⅓ cup semi sundried tomatoes
½ small red onion, sliced

1 Combine the PHILLY with the pesto then
spread on the base of the baguette. Top
with the spinach, chicken, tomatoes and
onion. Close with baguette top and cut
in half. Serve immediately.

Ham, Tomato & Basil on Chargrilled Turkish Bread

Makes 6
Preparation time: 5 minutes
Cooking time: 5 minutes

Olive oil spray
6 small Turkish bread rolls, sliced in half
300g sliced ham
½ cup basil leaves
3 medium tomatoes, thickly sliced
Salt and pepper, to taste
220g PHILADELPHIA Spreadable Extra Light
   Cream Cheese

1 Spray the Turkish bread lightly with the oil
and cook on a preheated chargrill plate for
2–3 minutes each side until golden.

2 Top each base with ham, basil and
tomato, season to taste. Spread the PHILLY
onto remaining bread halves, then close
and cut each roll in half. Serve immediately.

NB These sandwiches may be cooked in a heated
sandwich press for 4–5 minutes, if desired, in which
case there is no need to toast the rolls.

Spinach, Olive & Pine Nut Tart

Serves 6
Preparation time: 20 minutes
Cooking time: 45 minutes

2 sheets frozen shortcrust pastry, thawed
2 teaspoons olive oil

1 red onion, finely sliced
200g baby spinach leaves
1 cup pitted kalamata olives
125g PHILADELPHIA Block Cream Cheese,
   broken into 2cm pieces
4 eggs
½ cup cream
Salt and pepper, to taste
2 tablespoons pine nuts

Green salad, to serve

1 Press pastry into the base of a lightly greased 33cm x 9cm rectangular fluted tart pan with removable base. Pastry will need to overlap slightly and be trimmed to fit. Prick well with a fork and bake in a hot oven 200°C for 8–10 minutes until lightly golden. Allow to cool.

2 Heat the oil in a large frypan, add onion and sauté for 2–3 minutes until softened. Stir in spinach and olives, cook a further 1–2 minutes until spinach has just wilted. Cool slightly.

3 Spoon spinach mixture over the base of pastry and scatter over PHILLY chunks. Whisk together the eggs, cream and seasonings, then pour over spinach mixture. Top with pine nuts and bake in a moderately slow oven 160°C for 20–30 minutes until set. Slice and serve with green salad. Serve immediately.

Winter Vegetable Tartlets

Makes 6
Preparation time: 25 minutes
Cooking time: 50 minutes

500g butternut pumpkin, peeled and cut into small chunks
350g baby beetroot, washed and halved
Olive oil spray
1 leek, halved lengthways and thickly sliced

3 sheets frozen shortcrust pastry, thawed

125g PHILADELPHIA Block Cream Cheese, softened
¼ cup sour cream
2 eggs
1 clove garlic, crushed
Salt and pepper, to taste
2 tablespoons chopped thyme

Green salad, to serve

1 Place pumpkin and beetroot on a lined baking tray. Spray with oil and bake in a hot oven 200°C for 20 minutes. Add leek to the tray, spray with oil and continue cooking for a further 10–15 minutes until vegetables are tender.

2 Cut out 2 x 14cm rounds from each sheet of pastry and press into 6 greased 12cm round loose-based tartlet pans. Prick bases with a fork and bake in a hot oven 200°C for 8–10 minutes or until just starting to colour.

3 Whisk together the PHILLY, sour cream, eggs, garlic and seasonings until smooth. Pour PHILLY mixture evenly into the pastry cases, top with the roasted vegetables, sprinkle with thyme and bake in a hot oven 200°C for 12–15 minutes until filling is set. Place on serving plates with green salad. Serve immediately.

Capsicums with Tuna, Basil & Pine Nuts

Serves 4
Preparation time: 10 minutes
Cooking time: 25 minutes

4 medium yellow or red capsicums
2 × 95g cans tomato and onion flavoured tuna
125g PHILADELPHIA Block Cream Cheese,
    crumbled into small pieces
1 cup basil leaves, roughly chopped
½ cup fresh breadcrumbs
⅓ cup toasted pine nuts
Salt and pepper, to taste
Olive oil spray

Green salad, to serve

1 Slice the tops off the capsicums and discard seeds. Place capsicums on a lined baking tray, cut side up.

2 Mix together the tuna, PHILLY, basil, breadcrumbs, pine nuts and seasonings. Divide mixture evenly between the capsicums. Spray with oil.

3 Bake in a hot oven 200°C for 15 minutes, then replace capsicum tops and bake a further 5–10 minutes until tender. Place capsicums onto serving plates with green salad. Serve immediately.

Savoury Smoked Chicken Cheesecake

Serves 12
Preparation time: 25 minutes
Cooking time: 50 minutes

250g savoury cheese biscuits, crushed
90g butter, melted

20g butter, extra
2 large leeks, sliced
250g PHILADELPHIA Block Cream Cheese, softened
1¼ cups sour cream
5 eggs
200g smoked chicken breast, roughly chopped
1 cup semi sundried tomatoes, roughly chopped
1 cup grated tasty cheese
1 tablespoon chopped oregano
Salt and pepper, to taste

Green salad, to serve

1 Combine biscuit crumbs and butter and press into the base of a greased and lined 23cm springform pan. Chill.

2 Heat extra butter in a non–stick frypan and sauté leeks until softened. Cool. Beat PHILLY using an electric mixer until smooth. Beat in the sour cream then the eggs, one at a time, until well combined. Stir in the leek, chicken, tomatoes, cheese, oregano and seasonings.

3 Pour mixture into prepared base and bake in a moderately slow oven 160°C for 45–50 minutes or until just set. Cool slightly in oven with door ajar before removing from pan. Serve sliced, warm or cold with a green salad.

Spanish Style Chorizo Pizza

Makes 1 x 26cm pizza
Preparation time: 10 minutes
Cooking time: 15 minutes

1 x 26cm pizza base
¼ cup tomato paste or pizza sauce
90g PHILADELPHIA Block Cream Cheese, broken into 2cm pieces
1 roasted red capsicum, cut into thick strips
1 chorizo sausage, sliced diagonally
1 small red onion, sliced
Olive oil spray
50g rocket leaves

1 Spread the pizza base evenly with tomato paste then top with the PHILLY, capsicum, chorizo and onion. Spray with oil.

2 Bake the pizza in a hot oven 200°C for 10-15 minutes or until cooked through and PHILLY is golden brown.

3 Top with rocket leaves. Serve immediately.

Homemade Pizza Base

Makes 1 x 26cm pizza base
Preparation time: 10 minutes
Standing time: 20-30 minutes

1 cup plain flour, sifted
½ teaspoon caster sugar
¼ teaspoon salt
1 teaspoon dried yeast
⅓ cup lukewarm water
1 tablespoon oil

1 Combine in a bowl the flour, sugar, salt and yeast. Make a well in the centre of the dry ingredients and stir in the combined water and oil. Stir to form a soft dough.

2 Turn onto a floured surface and knead for 3-5 minutes. Place in a lightly greased bowl and cover with plastic wrap. Stand in a warm place for 20 to 30 minutes or until dough has doubled in size.

3 Roll out on a floured surface to form a 26cm round pizza base. Use as required.

Chicken Pizza with Avocado & Salsa

Makes 1 x 26cm pizza
Preparation time: 10 minutes
Cooking time: 15 minutes

1 x 26cm pizza base
125g PHILADELPHIA Spreadable Cream Cheese
1 small red onion, sliced
200g chicken tenderloins, cooked
Olive oil spray
⅓–½ cup tomato salsa
1 small avocado, sliced

1 Spread the pizza base evenly with the PHILLY then top with onion and chicken. Spray with oil.

2 Bake the pizza in a hot oven 200°C for 10–15 minutes or until cooked through and golden.

3 Top the pizza with salsa and avocado. Serve immediately.

Chilli Prawn Pizza

Makes 1 x 26cm pizza
Preparation time: 10 minutes
Cooking time: 15 minutes

1 x 26cm pizza base
125g PHILADELPHIA Spreadable Cream Cheese
12 green prawn cutlets
1 small red onion, sliced
Olive oil spray
⅓ cup sweet chilli sauce
Coriander leaves

1 Spread the pizza base evenly with the PHILLY then top with prawns and onion. Spray with oil.

2 Bake the pizza in a hot oven 200°C for 10–15 minutes or until base is golden and prawns are cooked through.

3 Drizzle pizza with sweet chilli sauce and sprinkle with coriander. Serve immediately.

Prosciutto & Basil Pizza

Serves 2
Preparation time: 5 minutes
Cooking time: 15 minutes

1 x 26cm pizza base
¼ cup tomato paste or pizza sauce
80g prosciutto
90g PHILADELPHIA Block Light Cream Cheese,
    broken into 2cm pieces
12 pitted black olives
6 cherry tomatoes, halved
Olive oil spray
Basil leaves, for serving

1 Spread the pizza base evenly with tomato paste then top with the prosciutto, PHILLY, olives and tomatoes. Spray with oil.

2 Bake the pizza in a hot oven 200°C for 10–15 minutes or until cooked through and PHILLY is golden brown.

3 Sprinkle the pizza with basil leaves. Serve immediately.

dinner

Leek, Asparagus & Mint Risotto

Serves 4
Preparation time: 15 minutes
Cooking time: 30 minutes

2 tablespoons oil
1 medium leek, sliced
1 small red capsicum, sliced
1 clove garlic, crushed
2 cups arborio rice
1 cup white wine
5 cups hot vegetable or chicken stock
1 bunch asparagus, cut into 3cm lengths
¼ cup chopped mint
125g PHILADELPHIA Block Cream Cheese,
    softened

1 Heat half the oil in a medium–large heavy based saucepan. Add leek and capsicum and sauté for 2–3 minutes until soft. Remove and set aside. Add the remaining oil, garlic and rice and stir for 1–2 minutes until translucent and well coated with oil. Add wine and cook until absorbed.

2 Gradually add the stock in small amounts, stirring occasionally until all the stock is absorbed and the rice is just tender.

3 Stir through the leek, capsicum, asparagus, mint and PHILLY, cook for a further 2–3 minutes until heated through. Spoon the risotto into serving bowls. Serve immediately.

Chicken & Shitake Mushroom Risotto

Serves 4

Preparation time: 10 minutes
Cooking time: 25 minutes

2 tablespoons oil
400g chicken tenderloins, cut into thick strips
250g shitake mushrooms
1 large onion, sliced
1 clove garlic, crushed
1½ cups arborio rice
½ cup white wine
4 cups hot chicken or vegetable stock
60g baby spinach
1 teaspoon finely grated lemon rind
125g PHILADELPHIA Spreadable Light
    Cream Cheese

Chives, for garnish

1 Heat half the oil in a medium–large heavy based saucepan and brown the chicken strips for 2–3 minutes then remove and set aside. Add the remaining oil, mushrooms, onion and garlic and sauté for 2–3 minutes. Remove the mushrooms and set aside.

2 Add the rice and stir for 1–2 minutes until translucent and well coated with oil. Add wine and cook until absorbed. Gradually add the stock in small amounts, stirring occasionally, until all the stock is absorbed and the rice is just tender.

3 Stir through the chicken, mushrooms, spinach, lemon rind, and PHILLY. Cook for a further 2–3 minutes until heated through. Spoon the risotto into serving bowls. Garnish with chives. Serve immediately.

Creamy Spaghetti Marinara

Serves 4
Preparation time: 15 minutes
Cooking time: 25 minutes

300g spaghetti

1½ cups chicken stock
¾ cup white wine
2 cloves garlic, crushed
125g PHILADELPHIA Block Cream Cheese,
    softened
1 tablespoon capers, chopped
1 tablespoon grated lemon rind
Salt and pepper, to taste
12 black mussels, scrubbed and beards removed
12 medium green prawn cutlets
12 large scallops, without roe
1 squid tube, sliced into rings
¼ cup roughly chopped flat leaf parsley

1 Cook the spaghetti in a large saucepan
of rapidly boiling water for 10–12 minutes until
al dente. Drain and keep warm.

2 Combine the stock, wine and garlic in
a medium saucepan, bring to the boil and
reduce by half. Add the PHILLY and whisk until
smooth, stir through the capers, lemon rind and
seasonings.

3 Add the mussels and prawns, cover and cook
for 2 minutes. Add the scallops and squid, cover
and cook a further 2–3 minutes until the seafood
is cooked. Stir through the spaghetti and parsley
and cook until heated through. Spoon the pasta
into serving bowls. Serve immediately.

Garlic & Chilli Prawns

Serves 4
Preparation time: 15 minutes
Cooking time: 15 minutes

30g butter
4 spring onions, diagonally sliced
3 cloves garlic, crushed
1–2 teaspoons finely shredded chilli
500g green prawn cutlets
250g PHILADELPHIA Spreadable Cream Cheese
½ cup fish or chicken stock

50g baby spinach leaves, to serve
Rice, to serve

1 Melt the butter in a large frypan and sauté the spring onions, garlic and chilli for 2–3 minutes. Add the prawns and continue cooking for 3–5 minutes until the prawns are cooked through.

2 Stir in the PHILLY and stock, simmer gently until the sauce is well combined and slightly thickened.

3 Place a bed of spinach into each serving bowl, top with the prawns and serve with rice. Serve immediately.

Crunchy Fish Pot Pie

Serves 6
Preparation time: 25 minutes
Cooking time: 30 minutes

1 tablespoon oil
1 leek, sliced
2 cloves garlic, crushed
1/3 cup flour
1½ cups fish or chicken stock
125g PHILADELPHIA Block Light Cream Cheese,
    softened
800g firm white fish fillets, cut into thick strips
Finely grated rind of 1 lemon
Salt and pepper, to taste

6 sheets filo pastry
Olive oil spray

Steamed vegetables, to serve

1 Heat oil in a large frypan, add leek and garlic and sauté 1–2 minutes until softened. Stir through the flour and cook for 1–2 minutes.

2 Combine the stock and PHILLY and add to the leek mixture, stirring until well combined. Bring to the boil, reduce heat and simmer for 5 minutes or until thickened. Add the fish, lemon rind and seasonings then remove from heat. Pour into a lightly oiled 8-cup capacity ovenproof baking dish.

3 Make a stack with three sheets of filo, spraying each layer with oil. Cut into 8 squares and scrunch up. Repeat process with remaining 3 sheets of filo. Place on top of the fish mixture and bake in a hot oven 200°C for 20 minutes or until pastry is golden. Spoon onto serving plates with green salad. Serve immediately.

Atlantic Salmon with Herbed Cream

Serves 4
Preparation time: 10 minutes
Cooking time: 4–5 minutes

1 tablespoon oil
4 Atlantic salmon fillets (approx 150g each), skin on
Salt and pepper, to taste

250g PHILADELPHIA Spreadable Light
   Cream Cheese
2 cloves garlic, crushed
2 tablespoons finely chopped herbs,
   e.g. parsley, chives, dill

Green salad, to serve
Dill, for garnish

1 Heat the oil in a non–stick frypan. Season
salmon with salt and pepper then place skin
side down and cook for 2 minutes each side
or until cooked to your liking. Remove from the
pan and rest for 2 minutes.

2 Combine the PHILLY with garlic and herbs
and mix well.

3 Place the salmon on serving plates with salad,
then top each with a dollop of herbed PHILLY,
garnish with dill. Serve immediately.

Moroccan Style Fish

Serves 4
Preparation time: 20 minutes
Cooking time: 20 minutes

40g butter
1 large onion, sliced
1 teaspoon cumin
1 teaspoon ground coriander
¼ teaspoon chilli powder
¼ teaspoon turmeric
600g firm white fish fillets, cut into 2cm thick slices
¾ cup white wine
125g PHILADELPHIA Spreadable Cream Cheese
½ cup chicken stock
3 teaspoons cornflour, blended with
   2 tablespoons water
Salt and pepper, to taste
1 tablespoon roughly chopped flat leaf parsley
1 tablespoon roughly chopped coriander

Rice, to serve
Steamed green vegetables, to serve

1 Melt the butter in a large frypan and sauté the onion for 4 minutes until softened, add the spices and cook a further minute. Add the fish and sauté for 4–5 minutes or until just cooked. Remove the fish from pan.

2 Pour the wine into the hot frypan, simmer until reduced slightly. Add combined PHILLY, stock and blended cornflour, stir until sauce boils and thickens. Return the fish to the pan, simmer gently for a further 5 minutes, season to taste.

3 Spoon the fish onto serving plates and sprinkle with combined herbs. Serve with rice and steamed green vegetables. Serve immediately.

Creamy Smoked Paprika Chicken

Serves 4

Preparation time: 10 minutes
Cooking time: 30 minutes

1 tablespoon oil
4 chicken fillets
1 large onion, sliced
2 cloves garlic, crushed
1 tablespoon flour
2 teaspoons smoked paprika
¾ cup chicken stock
1 x 400g can crushed tomatoes
125g PHILADELPHIA Spreadable Cream Cheese
Salt and pepper, to taste
2 tablespoons chopped parsley

Steamed vegetables, to serve

1 Heat half the oil in a non-stick frypan, add the chicken and cook 3–4 minutes each side until browned. Remove and set aside.

2 Heat remaining oil and sauté the onion and garlic for 3 minutes until softened. Add flour and paprika and cook a further minute. Stir in stock and tomatoes. Return chicken to the pan and simmer, covered, for 15 minutes or until the chicken is cooked through.

3 Whisk together the PHILLY with some of the cooking liquid until smooth, add to the pan with seasonings and parsley. Cook a further 2–3 minutes until heated through. Place chicken on serving plates, spoon over the sauce and serve with steamed vegetables. Serve immediately.

Bacon, Olive & Almond Filled Chicken

Serves 4
Preparation time: 15 minutes
Cooking time: 30 minutes

125g PHILADELPHIA Block Cream Cheese,
   crumbled
50g short cut rindless bacon, chopped
1/3 cup fresh breadcrumbs
1/4 cup pitted Kalamata olives, chopped
1/4 cup slivered almonds, roughly chopped
1 egg
1 tablespoon chopped oregano
Salt and pepper, to taste
4 chicken fillets
1 tablespoon oil
3/4 cup white wine
3/4 cup chicken stock
1 teaspoon cornflour, blended with
   1 tablespoon water

Roasted pumpkin, to serve
Steamed broccolini, to serve

1 Combine the PHILLY, bacon, breadcrumbs, olives, almonds, egg, oregano, and seasonings in a bowl. Carefully cut a pocket in each chicken fillet. Divide the filling evenly between the chicken fillets and press in firmly, secure with toothpicks.

2 Heat the oil in a large non-stick frypan, add the chicken and cook 3–4 minutes each side until browned. Remove and place in a greased baking dish. Cover and bake in a moderate oven 180°C for 15–20 minutes until cooked through. Allow to rest for 5 minutes.

3 Add the wine and stock to the frypan and simmer until reduced by a third, add the blended cornflour and any juices from the roasting pan, continue stirring until thickened. Slice the chicken and place on serving plates, spoon over the sauce and serve with pumpkin and broccolini. Serve immediately.

Roast Chicken with Creamy Herb Seasoning

Serves 4

Preparation time: 15 minutes
Cooking time: 1¼–1½ hours

1.5 kg whole chicken
1 cup chopped flat leaf parsley
½ cup chopped mint
¼ cup chopped rosemary
4 cloves garlic, chopped
1 lemon, rind finely grated and lemon cut in half
Salt and pepper, to taste
125g PHILADELPHIA Block Light Cream Cheese, softened
2 teaspoons olive oil
Salt flakes and pepper, to taste

Roasted vegetables, to serve

1 Wash the chicken under running water and pat dry with a paper towel. Lift the skin away from the breast meat to form a pocket underneath the skin.

2 Combine the herbs, garlic, lemon rind, seasonings and PHILLY. Carefully spread the mixture under the skin of the chicken to evenly cover the breast meat. Place lemon halves into cavity of the chicken and truss with string.

3 Rub the chicken with oil and sprinkle with salt flakes. Bake in a moderate oven 180°C, basting occasionally with pan juices for 1¼–1½ hours or until juices run clear when tested. Slice chicken and place on serving plates, serve with roasted vegetables and pan juices. Serve immediately.

Creamy Chicken & Thyme Penne

Serves 4
Preparation time: 10 minutes
Cooking time: 25 minutes

1 tablespoon oil
500g chicken tenderloins, halved
1 onion, finely chopped
1 clove garlic, crushed
50g pancetta or bacon, thinly sliced
¾ cup chicken stock
185ml can evaporated milk
125g PHILADELPHIA Spreadable Light
   Cream Cheese
½ cup semi sundried tomatoes
⅓ cup frozen peas
2 teaspoons chopped thyme
Salt and pepper, to taste
250g penne, cooked, drained, kept warm

1 Heat the oil in a non-stick frypan and cook chicken for 5–8 minutes or until golden. Remove and keep warm. Add the onions, garlic and pancetta to the pan and sauté for 2–3 minutes until the onions have softened.

2 Stir in the stock, milk and PHILLY, until combined. Return the chicken to the pan with the tomatoes, peas and thyme. Allow to simmer for a further 5–8 minutes until the sauce has slightly thickened and chicken is cooked through. Season to taste.

3 Divide the cooked pasta between the serving bowls and spoon over the sauce. Serve immediately.

Bacon, Mushroom & Basil Gnocchi

Serves 4
Preparation time: 15 minutes
Cooking time: 10 minutes

1 tablespoon oil
3 rashers bacon, sliced
200g button mushrooms, halved
1 red onion, sliced
250g PHILADELPHIA Block Light Cream Cheese
½–¾ cup milk
2 cloves garlic, crushed
½ cup basil leaves
500g gnocchi, cooked, drained, kept warm

Basil leaves extra, for garnish
Shaved Parmesan, to serve

1 Heat the oil in a large non-stick frypan and cook bacon, mushrooms and onion until browned. Add the PHILLY, milk and garlic, stir until smooth then simmer for 2–3 minutes.

2 Add the gnocchi to the pan and toss through the sauce. Reheat gently for 2–3 minutes then stir through basil leaves. Spoon the gnocchi into serving bowls and garnish with extra basil leaves and Parmesan. Serve immediately.

Fruit & Macadamia Pork with Port Sauce

Serves 6
Preparation time: 30 minutes
Cooking time: 30 minutes

125g PHILADELPHIA Block Cream Cheese,
    softened
½ cup dried fruit medley
¼ cup chopped macadamia nuts
Salt and pepper, to taste
4 pork fillets (approx 250g each)
50g baby spinach leaves
2 tablespoons oil

1 cup port
½ cup chicken stock
2 teaspoons cornflour, blended with
    1 tablespoon water

1 bunch watercress, trimmed, to serve
Steamed baby squash, to serve

1 Combine PHILLY, fruit, nuts and seasonings. Make a cut lengthways down the centre of each pork fillet, ¾ of the way through the fillet. Place spinach leaves down the centre of each open fillet then spoon the PHILLY mixture over spinach. Fold the fillet over to enclose the filling and secure with toothpicks.

2 Heat the oil in a large frypan and brown pork fillets on all sides. Transfer to a baking dish and bake in a moderate oven 180°C for 20 minutes or until cooked through.

3 Remove fillets from baking dish, wrap in foil and rest for 10 minutes. Combine pork juices, port and stock in baking dish and bring to the boil, stirring to loosen all pan juices. Add blended cornflour and cook for 3–4 minutes or until slightly thickened. Slice pork and place on serving plates, drizzle with sauce and serve with watercress and baby squash. Serve immediately.

Mediterranean Meatballs with Couscous

Serves 6
Preparation time: 15 minutes
Cooking time: 30 minutes

500g pork and veal mince
125g PHILADELPHIA Spreadable Cream Cheese
1 onion, finely chopped
2 cloves garlic, crushed
1 egg
2 cups fresh breadcrumbs
½ cup stuffed green olives, finely chopped
1 tablespoon finely chopped oregano
 Salt and pepper, to taste

1 tablespoon oil
800g can chopped tomatoes
1 cup chicken stock
1 teaspoon brown sugar

Couscous, to serve
Crusty bread, to serve

1 Combine the mince, PHILLY, onion, garlic, egg, breadcrumbs, olives, oregano and seasonings in a large bowl. Shape mixture into 24 meatballs.

2 Heat oil in a large non-stick frypan, and cook the meatballs in 2 batches, for 5 minutes each or until browned. Return all meatballs to pan. Add tomatoes, stock and sugar, bring to the boil then simmer uncovered for 15–20 minutes.

3 Spoon the meatballs onto a bed of couscous on serving plates and drizzle with sauce. Serve with crusty bread. Serve immediately.

Scotch Fillet with Pepper & Mushroom Sauce

Serves 4
Preparation time: 10 minutes
Cooking time: 15 minutes

Olive oil spray
4 thick cut scotch fillet steaks

60g butter
4 x 8cm flat mushrooms, stalks trimmed
2 cloves garlic, crushed
1 teaspoon coarse ground black pepper
1 cup beef stock
2 tablespoons brandy
125g PHILADELPHIA Spreadable Light
    Cream Cheese
1 teaspoon brown sugar

Thick cut chips, to serve
Steamed bok choy, to serve

1 Heat a non-stick frypan over a high heat. Spray the steaks with oil and cook for 2–3 minutes each side, or to your liking. Remove from the pan, wrap in foil and keep warm.

2 Reduce heat and melt half the butter, add the mushrooms and sauté for 2–3 minutes each side. Remove and keep warm.

3 Add the remaining butter to the pan and sauté the garlic and pepper for 1 minute. Pour in the stock and brandy and simmer until reduced by a third.

4 Whisk in the PHILLY and brown sugar and simmer until slightly thickened. Place the steaks on heated serving plates, top each with a mushroom then spoon over the sauce. Serve with thick cut chips and bok choy. Serve immediately.

Slow Cooked Beef & Red Wine Ragout

Serves 6–8
Preparation time: 15 minutes
Cooking time: 2 hours

¼ cup oil
1kg pickling onions, peeled and halved
1kg chuck steak or gravy beef, cut into chunks
2 cloves garlic, crushed
⅓ cup tomato paste
2 cups beef stock
1 cup red wine
125g PHILADELPHIA Block Light Cream Cheese
Salt and pepper, to taste

Cooked pasta, to serve

1 Heat half the oil in a large heavy based saucepan and cook the onions until browned. Set aside. Heat remaining oil and brown beef in batches. Set aside.

2 Add garlic and tomato paste and gently cook for 1 minute. Return beef to saucepan, add stock and wine and bring to the boil. Reduce heat, cover and simmer for 1½ hours, stirring occasionally. Add onions and cook a further 20 minutes.

3 Whisk together the PHILLY with some of the cooking liquid until smooth, add to the saucepan and simmer a further 10 minutes. Spoon onto serving plates with pasta. Serve immediately.

Chargrilled Lamb
with Cream Cheese Polenta

Serves 4
Preparation time: 20 minutes
Cooking time: 30 minutes

500–600g lamb backstraps
Olive oil spray

½ cup red wine
¼ cup balsamic vinegar
¼ cup honey
1 clove garlic, crushed
2 sprigs of thyme or rosemary

2 cups water
1½ cups milk
1 cup instant polenta
125g PHILADELPHIA Block Light Cream Cheese
¼ cup grated Parmesan cheese
Salt and pepper, to taste

Chargrilled vegetables, to serve
Sprigs of thyme, for garnish

1 Spray the lamb with oil and chargrill for 3 minutes each side. Wrap in foil and keep warm.

2 Combine the wine, vinegar, honey, garlic and thyme in a saucepan, bring to the boil, then simmer 5 minutes or until slightly thickened and a little syrupy. Keep warm.

3 Bring the water and milk to the boil in a medium–large saucepan. Reduce heat and whisk in the polenta. Continue to whisk for 4–5 minutes or until the mixture comes away from the sides of the saucepan. Remove from heat and whisk in PHILLY, Parmesan and seasonings.

4 Divide polenta between serving plates, top with chargrilled vegetables and slices of lamb. Drizzle with the sauce and garnish with thyme sprigs. Serve immediately.

Glazed Veal Cutlets with Chive Mash

Serves 4
Preparation time: 20 minutes
Cooking time: 30 minutes

2 large (600g) potatoes, peeled and chopped
125g PHILADELPHIA Spreadable Cream Cheese
¼ cup milk
2 tablespoons chopped chives
Salt and pepper, to taste

2 tablespoons chopped rosemary
3 cloves garlic, crushed
2 tablespoons oil
Salt and pepper, to taste
4 veal cutlets
½ cup beef stock
⅓ cup redcurrant jelly
2 tablespoons red wine vinegar

Steamed asparagus, to serve

1 Boil the potatoes in a medium saucepan for 10–15 minutes or until tender. Drain and mash with the PHILLY and milk. Stir through the chives then season to taste. Keep warm.

2 Combine the rosemary, garlic, oil and seasonings. Rub half of the mix over the cutlets. Cook the cutlets in a large non-stick frypan over a high heat for 3 minutes each side or until cooked to your liking. Remove and wrap in foil. Keep warm.

3 Reduce the heat then add the remaining herb and garlic mixture to the pan and cook gently for 1 minute. Pour in the stock, redcurrant jelly and vinegar, simmer until reduced by one third. Spoon the mash onto serving plates, top with the cutlets, drizzle with glaze and serve with asparagus. Serve immediately.

dessert

Baked Apples with Creamy Vanilla Bean Custard

Serves 4

Preparation time: 15 minutes
Cooking time: 30 minutes

4 Pink Lady apples
1 cup dessert wine
1 cinnamon stick
¼ cup brown sugar

250g PHILADELPHIA Spreadable Cream Cheese, softened
½ cup milk
¼ cup caster sugar
1 vanilla bean, split
1 tablespoon custard powder, blended with 2 tablespoons milk, to form a paste

1 Cut each apple horizontally into three slices, place in a large shallow baking dish with the wine and cinnamon. Sprinkle over the brown sugar. Bake in a moderate oven 180°C for 20 minutes until tender. Spoon the syrup over the apples occasionally.

2 Whisk together the PHILLY and milk in a saucepan until smooth. Add the sugar, vanilla bean and custard powder paste. Bring to the boil, stirring until custard has thickened, discard the vanilla bean.

3 Remove apples from syrup and arrange on serving plates, then pour over the custard. Serve immediately.

Fresh Berries with Honey Cream Cheese

Serves 4

Preparation time: 10 minutes

220g PHILADELPHIA Spreadable Extra Light
   Cream Cheese
2 tablespoons honey

2–3 punnets fresh berries e.g. raspberries,
   strawberries, blueberries

Mint sprigs, for decoration
Almond bread, to serve

1 Combine the PHILLY and honey in a bowl,
stir until smooth.

2 Spoon half the PHILLY into 4 serving glasses.
Top with the berries. Dollop over the remaining
PHILLY and decorate with mint. Serve with almond
bread. Serve immediately.

Peaches & Cream Cheese Mille Feuille

Serves 6
Preparation time: 10 minutes
Cooking time: 10 minutes

4 sheets filo pastry
Olive oil spray

⅓ cup brown sugar
2 teaspoons vanilla
825g can peach slices, drained

250g PHILADELPHIA Spreadable Light
   Cream Cheese
¼ cup pure icing sugar, sifted

Icing sugar, extra, for dusting

1 Spray each sheet of filo with oil and stack on top of each other. Cut into 12 even rectangles. Place on a lined oven tray and bake in a hot oven 200°C for 4–5 minutes or until crisp and golden. Cool on a wire rack.

2 Heat the brown sugar and vanilla in a non-stick frypan stirring until dissolved. Add peaches and cook a further minute until coated. Allow to cool.

3 Combine the PHILLY and sugar. Place one filo rectangle on a serving plate, gently spread with the PHILLY and top with peaches. Place another filo rectangle on top. Repeat with remaining filo, PHILLY and peaches to make 6 stacks. Dust with icing sugar. Serve immediately.

Red Wine Poached Pears with Orange & Pistachio Cream

Serves 6

Preparation time: 20 minutes
Cooking time: 35 minutes

2 cups red wine
2 cups water
½ cup caster sugar
2 x 5cm pieces orange rind
2 star anise
6 Beurre Bosc pears, peeled, halved and cored

250g PHILADELPHIA Spreadable Light
   Cream Cheese
¼ cup orange juice
2 tablespoons finely chopped pistachio nuts
¼ cup caster sugar, extra
1 teaspoon finely grated orange rind

Pistachio nuts, extra, for decoration

1 Combine the wine, water, sugar, orange rind and star anise in a large saucepan and bring to the boil. Reduce heat and simmer for 5 minutes. Add the pears and simmer for 20 minutes until tender. Remove pears and allow to cool. Simmer the liquid until reduced by half. Cool.

2 Combine PHILLY, orange juice, nuts, extra sugar and orange rind. Place 2 pear halves on each serving plate. Dollop with pistachio cream, drizzle with syrup and sprinkle over extra nuts. Serve immediately.

Layered Apricot & Ginger Creams

Serves 4
Preparation time: 10 minutes

220g PHILADELPHIA Spreadable Extra Light
  Cream Cheese
¼ cup caster sugar
1 teaspoon grated lemon rind

12 gingernut biscuits, roughly broken
825g can apricot halves, drained and pureed

1 Combine the PHILLY, sugar and lemon rind.
Spoon a third of the mixture into 4 serving glasses.

2 Place half the broken gingernuts over the
PHILLY then spoon half the apricot puree over
the top. Continue to layer the desserts with
another third of PHILLY and the remaining biscuits
and fruit. Top with the remaining PHILLY.

3 Refrigerate for 2–3 hours or until the biscuits
have softened. Serve immediately.

Light & Creamy Savoiardi Frames

Serves 4
Preparation time: 20 minutes

6 sponge finger biscuits (Savoiardi),
    halved lengthways
100g dark chocolate, melted

220g PHILADELPHIA Spreadable Extra Light
    Cream Cheese
¼ cup pure icing sugar, sifted
1 teaspoon vanilla

Fresh fruit, for serving e.g. berries, mango,
    peaches, kiwi fruit
Icing sugar, for dusting

1 Coat both ends of three sponge finger halves
in chocolate. Place the pieces on a lined tray
to form a triangular shape. Ensure the chocolate
ends are overlapping as these will secure the
frames once the chocolate has set. Repeat with
remaining biscuits and chocolate to form four
triangular frames. Allow to set.

2 Combine the PHILLY with the icing sugar
and vanilla.

3 Arrange frames on individual serving plates.
Fill the centre of each with a dollop of PHILLY,
fresh fruit and a dusting of icing sugar.
Serve immediately.

Espresso & Vanilla Panna Cotta

Serves 4
Preparation time: 25 minutes
Cooking time: 10 minutes

¼ cup espresso coffee
¼ cup sugar

1 cup cream
¼ cup caster sugar
½ vanilla bean, split
250g PHILADELPHIA Block Cream Cheese,
   softened
1 teaspoon gelatine, dissolved in 1 tablespoon
   boiling water and cooled

Biscotti, to serve

1 Combine coffee and sugar in a small saucepan
and stir until sugar is dissolved. Simmer for 1–2 minutes
or until thick and syrupy. Pour into 4 x ½ cup espresso
glasses, allow to cool.

2 Heat the cream, sugar and vanilla bean in a
saucepan until almost boiling. (Do not allow to
boil.) Discard vanilla bean and cool the mixture.
Beat PHILLY with an electric mixer until smooth then
gradually beat in the cream mixture and gelatine.

3 Spoon the PHILLY mixture into the glasses and
refrigerate for 2–3 hours or until set. Place glasses
onto espresso saucers with biscotti on the side.
Serve immediately.

Cookies & Cream Slice

Serves 15
Preparation time: 20 minutes
Cooking time: 5 minutes

350g OREO Original Cookies
80g butter, melted

375g PHILADELPHIA Block Cream Cheese,
   softened
½ cup caster sugar
1 teaspoon vanilla
1 cup cream
3 teaspoons gelatine, dissolved in ¼ cup
   boiling water
200g white chocolate, melted, cooled slightly

Strawberries, for decoration
Extra OREO Original Cookies, broken for
   decoration, if desired

1 Place 250g of the OREO cookies in a food
processor and process into fine crumbs. Add
the butter and process to combine. Press the
mixture into a greased and lined 18cm x 28cm
slice pan and chill.

2 Beat the PHILLY, sugar and vanilla with an
electric mixer until smooth, then beat in the cream.
Stir through the gelatine and white chocolate.

3 Roughly chop the remaining cookies and
stir through the filling, then pour over the OREO
cookie base. Refrigerate 3 hours or until set.
Cut into triangles and decorate with strawberries
and extra OREO cookies. Serve immediately.

Creamy TOBLERONE Froth

Serve 6
Preparation time: 20 minutes
Cooking time: 5 minutes

200g TOBLERONE Milk Chocolate,
    roughly chopped
250g PHILADELPHIA Spreadable Light
    Cream Cheese
2 eggs, separated
1–2 tablespoons coffee liqueur, optional

18 red grapes
18 strawberries
3 kiwi fruit, cut into chunks

1 Melt chocolate in a heat proof bowl over simmering water. Allow to cool.

2 Whisk the PHILLY, egg yolks and liqueur together until smooth then stir through the chocolate. Beat the egg whites with an electric beater until stiff peaks form; gently fold into the chocolate mixture. Pour into a serving dish. Refrigerate 1 hour or until firm.

3 Thread pieces of fruit onto 18 short bamboo skewers. Serve TOBLERONE Froth on a large platter with skewers. Serve immediately.

Coffee Liqueur Cheesecake

Serves 10
Preparation time: 20 minutes

1¼ cups sweet biscuit crumbs
80g butter, melted

500g PHILADELPHIA Block Cream Cheese,
    softened
¾ cup caster sugar
2 tablespoons coffee liqueur
3 teaspoons gelatine, dissolved in ¼ cup
    boiling water
2 teaspoons instant coffee, dissolved in
1 tablespoon boiling water
1 cup cream, lightly whipped

Double cream, to serve
Chocolate curls, to decorate

1 Combine biscuit crumbs and butter.
Press into the base of a greased 20cm
springform pan. Chill.

2 Beat the PHILLY and sugar using an electric
mixer until smooth. Add the coffee liqueur,
gelatine and coffee and beat until well
combined, then gently fold in the whipped
cream.

3 Pour into the prepared base and refrigerate
3 hours or until set. Slice the cheesecake, top
with a dollop of cream and chocolate curls.
Serve immediately.

Lime Cream Cheese Frosting

To ice a 22cm loaf or 20–23cm cake
Preparation time: 10 minutes

250g PHILADELPHIA Block Cream Cheese, softened
2/3 cup icing sugar mixture, sifted
2/3 cup full cream milk powder
Grated rind of 1 lime

1 Beat the PHILLY and sugar with an electric beater until smooth. Add the milk powder and beat again until smooth. Stir through the lime rind. Chill. Use as required.

Chocolate Peanut Frosting

To ice 12 muffins or cupcakes
Preparation time: 10 minutes

180g PHILADELPHIA Block Cream Cheese, softened
2 tablespoons smooth peanut butter
½ cup icing sugar mixture, sifted
150g milk chocolate, melted and cooled

1 Combine the PHILLY, peanut butter and sugar and stir until smooth. Gently fold through the melted chocolate. Use as required.

NB DO NOT beat or over mix.

Berry Clafoutis

Serves 4
Preparation time: 15 minutes
Cooking time: 20 minutes

1 tablespoon caster sugar
2 punnets raspberries or blueberries

125g PHILADELPHIA Block Light Cream Cheese
¾ cup caster sugar, extra
¼ cup flour, sifted
1 teaspoon vanilla
3 eggs
½ cup milk

Icing sugar, for dusting

1 Sprinkle sugar over the base of 4x1 cup capacity greased shallow ovenproof dishes. Divide berries evenly between the dishes.

2 Beat the PHILLY, extra sugar and flour with an electric beater until smooth. Gradually add the combined vanilla, eggs and milk, beat until smooth. Pour mixture evenly over berries.

3 Bake in a hot oven 200°C for 20 minutes or until golden and cooked, dust with icing sugar. Serve immediately.

Dark Chocolate
Bread & Butter Pudding

Serves 6–8
Preparation time: 15 minutes
Cooking time: 35 minutes

2½ cups milk
200g dark chocolate, roughly chopped
125g PHILADELPHIA Block Cream Cheese,
   softened
1 tablespoon cocoa
1 tablespoon caster sugar
4 eggs
8 slices raisin bread

Icing sugar, for dusting
Pure cream, to serve

1 Combine the milk, chocolate, PHILLY, cocoa and sugar in a large saucepan over low heat, stirring until smooth. Allow to cool then whisk in the eggs.

2 Cut each bread slice in half diagonally. Arrange bread triangles in a greased 2 litre capacity shallow baking dish. Pour over chocolate mixture and stand for 10 minutes.

3 Bake in a moderately slow oven 160°C for 35–40 minutes or until set. Allow to cool slightly. Dust with icing sugar and serve with cream. Serve immediately.

Summer Plum Tart

Serves 8
Preparation time: 20 minutes
Cooking time: 45 minutes

125g butter, melted
16 (200g) sponge finger biscuits (Savoiardi)

125g PHILADELPHIA Block Cream Cheese,
  softened
50g butter, extra, softened
¾ cup caster sugar
1 teaspoon vanilla
3 eggs
¼ cup flour
8–9 ripe plums, halved, stones removed

1 tablespoon caster sugar, extra
Cream, to serve

1 Place butter and biscuits in a food processor
and process until mixture resembles fine
breadcrumbs. Press firmly into the base and
sides of a 28cm round loose based flan tin.

2 Beat the PHILLY, extra butter, sugar and vanilla
using an electric beater until pale and fluffy.
Beat in eggs, one at a time, until well combined.
Add flour and beat until smooth.

3 Pour mixture over base then arrange the plums,
cut side down, over the filling. Sprinkle with extra
sugar and bake in a moderately hot oven 190°C
for 40 minutes or until golden, cool slightly and
remove from pan. Slice and serve warm or cold
with cream.

Sticky Date Cheesecake Slice with Caramel Fudge Sauce

Serves 8
Preparation time: 25 minutes
Cooking time: 30 minutes

100g butternut snap biscuits, crushed
20g butter, melted

375g PHILADELPHIA Block Cream Cheese, softened
⅓ cup caster sugar
1 teaspoon vanilla
1 egg
2 teaspoons plain flour
5 (125g) fresh dates, chopped

1 cup brown sugar, firmly packed
80g butter, extra
⅓ cup cream

Cream, extra, to serve

1 Combine the biscuit crumbs and butter in a bowl. Press mixture into the base of a greased and lined 9cm x 20cm loaf pan. Chill.

2 Beat the PHILLY, sugar and vanilla with an electric mixer until smooth. Beat in the egg then stir through the flour and dates. Pour filling into prepared base and bake in a moderately slow oven 160°C for 25 minutes or until just set. Cool in the oven with door ajar. Chill.

3 Combine brown sugar, extra butter and cream in a small saucepan, stirring over a low heat 5 minutes until thickened. Cut the cheesecake into thick slices and place on serving plates with a drizzle of sauce and a dollop of cream. Serve immediately.

See handy tips section for further advice on baking cheesecakes.

Strawberry & Cream Cheese Friands

Makes 12
Preparation time: 20 minutes
Cooking time: 25 minutes

125g PHILADELPHIA Block Cream Cheese,
   softened
80g butter, melted
1½ cups pure icing sugar, sifted
6 egg whites, lightly whisked
1¼ cups almond meal
½ cup plain flour, sifted with
½ teaspoon baking powder

12 strawberries, thinly sliced

1 Beat together the PHILLY, butter and icing
sugar until combined. Add the egg whites,
almond meal, flour and baking powder and
beat until smooth.

2 Spoon the mixture into 12 greased and base
lined friand pans. Top with strawberry slices and
bake in a moderate oven 180°C for 20–25 minutes
or until cooked and golden. Allow to stand in
pans 5 minutes before turning out onto a wire
rack. Serve warm or cold.

Iced Lemon Pound Cake

Serves 12
Preparation time: 20 minutes
Cooking time: 45–60 minutes

250g PHILADELPHIA Block Cream Cheese,
  softened
1¾ cups caster sugar
2 teaspoons vanilla
2 eggs
1 cup oil
2 cups self-raising flour, sifted
Grated rind of 2 lemons
Juice of 1 lemon

1 cup icing sugar mixture, sifted
Juice of 1 small lemon, extra

Lemon threads, for decoration if desired

1 Beat the PHILLY, sugar and vanilla with an electric mixer until smooth. Gradually beat in the eggs and oil then stir in the flour, lemon rind and juice, mix well.

2 Pour the mixture into a greased 25cm non-stick fluted ring pan. Bake in a moderate oven 180°C for 45–55 minutes or until cooked when tested with a skewer. Allow to cool for 5 minutes in the pan before turning onto a wire rack to cool.

3 Combine the icing sugar with enough lemon juice to form a thin icing. Drizzle over the cake and allow to set. Decorate with lemon threads if desired.

Cherry Yoghurt Cheesecake

Serves 10
Preparation time: 20 minutes
Cooking time: 35 minutes

1¼ cups sweet biscuit crumbs
80g butter, melted

750g PHILADELPHIA Block Cream Cheese,
   softened
¾ cup caster sugar
1½ teaspoons vanilla
2 eggs

200g Greek natural yoghurt

400g jar cherries, drained, liquid reserved
¼ cup caster sugar, extra
2 teaspoons arrowroot, blended with
1 tablespoon cold water

1 Combine biscuit crumbs and butter. Press into the base of a greased and lined 22cm round springform pan. Chill.

2 Beat 500g PHILLY, ½ cup sugar and 1 teaspoon vanilla using an electric mixer until smooth. Beat in the eggs, one at a time. Pour into the prepared base and bake in a moderate oven 180°C for 20 minutes. Cool 5 minutes.

3 Beat the remaining PHILLY, sugar and vanilla until smooth, then beat in the yoghurt. Pour over cooked base then bake for a further 10–15 minutes until just a little wobbly in centre. Allow to cool in oven with door ajar. Chill.

4 Combine the reserved cherry liquid, extra sugar and arrowroot mixture in a small saucepan and stir over a low heat until sugar has dissolved and syrup has thickened. Stir in cherries and cool. Slice the cheesecake and place onto serving plates, spoon over cherries and syrup. Serve immediately.

Mini Blueberry & Maple Cheesecakes

Makes 12
Preparation time: 25 minutes
Cooking time: 35 minutes

2 cups sweet biscuit crumbs
100g butter, melted

375g PHILADELPHIA Block Cream Cheese,
   softened
½ cup caster sugar
3 eggs
½ cup sour cream
¼ cup pure maple syrup
150g blueberries, fresh or frozen

Icing sugar, for dusting
Extra blueberries, to serve

1 Combine biscuit crumbs and butter. Press into the base of 12 × ⅓ cup capacity greased and base lined muffin pans. Chill.

2 Beat the PHILLY and sugar using an electric mixer until smooth. Add the eggs, sour cream and maple syrup and beat until well combined.

3 Pour the mixture into prepared pans and sprinkle over blueberries. Bake in a moderately slow oven 160°C for 35 minutes. Allow to cool in pans before removing. Place onto serving plates, dust with icing sugar and serve with extra berries. Serve immediately.

See handy tips section for further advice on baking cheesecakes.

White Chocolate & Hazelnut Ball

Serves 8
Preparation time: 10 minutes
Cooking time: 10 minutes

250g PHILADELPHIA Block Cream Cheese,
    softened
100g white chocolate, melted
1 tablespoon caster sugar

1 cup chopped roasted hazelnuts

Ginger biscuits, to serve
Chocolate chip bread, to serve

1 Combine PHILLY, chocolate and sugar
in a small bowl. Chill for 1 hour or until firm.
2 Form into 2 balls and coat in hazelnuts.
Chill until firm. Place onto 2 serving plates
and serve with ginger biscuits and
chocolate chip bread.

handy tips

To soften PHILADELPHIA Block Cream Cheese

We recommend that PHILADELPHIA Cream Cheese be softened before use. Allow to stand for one hour at room temperature, or remove PHILLY from foil, place in a microwave on high for 30 seconds per 250g.

When using PHILADELPHIA Light Cream Cheese

We recommend that PHILADELPHIA light Cream Cheese be softened before use and lightly beaten to incorporate other ingredients.

When using PHILADELPHIA Spreadable Cream Cheese

Mix spreadable gently with other ingredients until just combined. Do not over mix, or texture may thin as a result.

Baked Cheesecake tips

Avoid over beating the cream cheese or beating the cream cheese at high speed. Over beating incorporates air into the batter, causing the cheesecake to puff up and then collapse.

The best position for a cheesecake in the oven is the lowest shelf in a gas oven. If using an electric oven, position the cheesecake on the centre rack, well clear of the heating elements. For fan forced ovens reduce the temperature by 20°C.

Provide a moist baking environment for your cheesecake by placing a small bowl of hot tap water on the bottom of the oven. The steaming effect created helps prevent burning and the drying out of the cake crumbs.

Avoid over baking. A cheesecake is cooked when the edges are slightly puffed and the centre is slightly soft and custard like.

Allow baked cheesecakes to cool in the oven with the door ajar before refrigerating.

index

appetisers & salads

light meals

dinner

dessert

notes

acknowledgements

The PHILADELPHIA team would like to thank
everyone who was involved in the making
of this *Simply Heaven* Cookbook

Recipe Development and Food Styling

Trish McKenzie, Kraft Kitchens Manager with
the support of Melanie Ryan and Pam Tannourji

Photography

Louis Petruccelli and assistant Hayden Golder
along with retoucher Ernie Gal

Marketing Team

Jenna Hockey, Sarah Fagan and Paul Lamble

Thanks also go to: JWT for art direction.

The team at Lithocraft Pty Ltd and Collier & Associates
who helped this project come to life with the design,
layout and printing.